APRAN PROGRAMMING DANS PYTHON (LEARN PROGRAMMING IN PYTHON)

Yeeshtdevisingh Hosanee

(English Version)

Acknowledgement

Special thanks go to Kavish Chooramun for his tremendous input during the whole publication process of this book. The author wishes to also thank her family, Dr Panchoo, Priya, Ana, Nadine, Nilakshi, Phaly, Purmeshwar, Mousaffar, Valerie, Sandra, Patrice, Jaleela and her friends and colleagues for their continuous encouragement in relation to the publication of this book.

Printed in Mauritius

First Edition, 2021 (mycoding.fun Series)

ISBN: 978-99949-0-865-3 (registered in Mauritius)

Publisher: INDEPENDENT PUBLISHER

Reviewed By:

1. Proofers Ltd, United Kingdom (UK)
2. Priya Dookee
3. Kavish Chooramun

Table of Contents

List of Figures

List of Tables

1 Introduction

This book is written for students who are at least seven years old and who want to learn computer programming. It is also meant for any person wishing to expand his or her knowledge of computer programming. Parents may assist their children, if required.

The basic concepts of programming are explained in the first four sections of this book. Twenty practical questions and their expected results in Python programming language, are given and explained in the fifth section of this book.

Once the basic concepts of programming have been acquired, the learner will be able to proceed with other programming languages which have similar structures to Python langauge, though different grammatical rules.

2 What is computer programming?

Computer programming is a process where a person will use a keyboard to instruct a computing machine to perform a particular task by typing sentences, which are also known as lines of codes. When these lines of codes are executed, a computer program is formed.

A mobile phone, a computer, or a washing machine are three examples of computing machines. Displaying the sum of two numbers on a screen, executing a washing machine or switching on/off a mobile phone are examples of tasks performed by these computing machines.

3 Python programming language

Python, a high-level programming language, was designed in 1991 by Guido van Rossum. A high-level programming language consists of alphabetical letters and punctuation marks. A low-level programming language consists of only a series of 0's and 1's, compared to high-level language where the language is human readable.

4 Procedural Programming

Today, there are many types of programming. The one that we will be learning about in this book is procedural programming. The language we shall be using is the Python programming language.

You can download the Python software from the internet at https://www.Python.org/downloads/ and follow the installation instructions, or you can also look for an online Python editor to support your learning:

https://www.jdoodle.com/Python3-programming-online/

5 Concepts in computer programming

There are five main concepts in procedural programming: variables, arrays, conditional statements (if-then, else), repetitions, and functions. Other concepts include comments, indentation, pre-built functionalities, algorithm, and concatenation.

Comments: Any descriptive comments can be written in Python by adding the character **#** at the beginning of any line of code.

Indentation: To group codes under a particular concept or section, we often use a series of blank spaces at the start of a line of code. This is known as "indentation."

For example:

```
def draw():
```

print("drawing") #indentation is adding some blank spaces before typing line *print("drawing").* Note that line *def draw()* does not contain any blank space.

Pre-built functionalities: Python provides in-built functionalities (i.e., libraries) that can be imported using the keyword "import."

Algorithm: Before writing codes, the programming logic can be written in the English language to detail out the different steps in sequential order.

Concatenation: is a process where you can add at most two words together to form a single word (two set of characters "Tues" and "Day", when concatenated become one single word "TuesDay").

5.1 Variables

Variables are the unique identifiers given to a program. Each of them is defined by a unique name. A variable contains one value at a time. Integer and string, two datatypes, are two examples that define the type of value of a variable.

For example, **a="5"**, where **a** is a variable name in Python and the value of variable **a** is "5". In Python, when a value is in either double or single quotes, it is a text character (i.e., a String type).

If variable **a** was declared without quotes, as in **a=5**, the value 5, becomes an integer value.

5.2 Arrays

An array is a variable that can contain more than one value in a program.

For example: a=[4,5,6,7]

The above statement shows that array **a** contains four values: 4,5,6, and 7.

5.3 Conditional statements

Conditional statements are important in any program because they define the true and false possibility of an event. For example, if you want to go to Port-Louis city, you have the option either to opt for a car or a bus. Conditional statements with "if" and "else" statements allow you to write this code logic in your program. If a car is available for you, you will use "if statement" in your program. If no car is available for you, you will use the "else" part of your statement, indicating you would rather take a bus to go to the city.

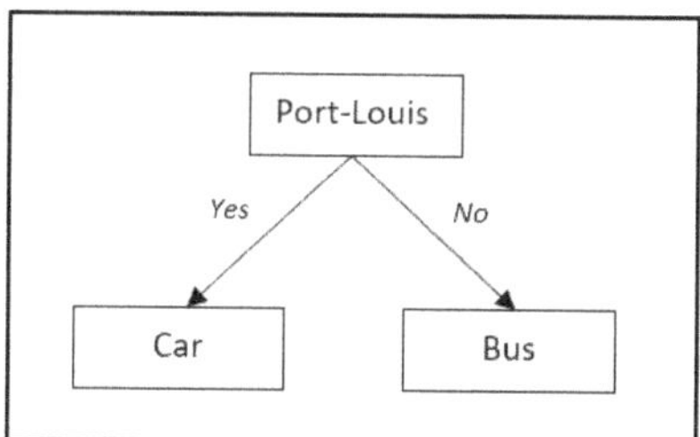

Figure 1 Conditional statements

Python codes:

```
a="car"
if a=="car": #if variable a is equal to "car"
value, then program goes inside the block
    print("Port-Louis by car")
else: # if no car is available, bus is taken
    print ("Port-Louis by bus")
```

Figure 2 if-else statements

5.4 Repetitions or Iterations

Iterations or repetitions are also known as loops or cycles. If you wish to read the different values of an array, you may use either a "for loop" or a "while loop" to achieve this.

Example 1 with a "for loop":

```
marks=[34,5,95,34]
for i in marks:
    if i>90: # if marks from the array list is
greater than 90
            print(i)    #    then    print    the
corresponding mark greater than 90
```

Figure 3 for loop codes

If you expect a program to display the marks which are greater than 90 on the screen, you can write the following program:

In the above example, the different marks are stored in the array **marks** with the following values: 34,5,95, 34.

The statement "for i in marks:" will start a looping process. The array "marks" will be read one value at a time. Each value from the array will be assigned to the variable "i". In the first loop, the variable "i" will contain value 34. In the second loop, the variable "i", will contain the value 5. In the third loop, the variable "i" will contain the value 95, and in the fourth loop, the variable "i" will contain the value 34.

On each loop, there will be a conditional statement, verifying if the value of the mark is greater than 90. In the third loop, the condition is matched as mark "95" is greater than 90. Among the four given marks (34,5,95, and 34) in the array

marks, only value **95** met the condition of **if i>90** and **95** is displayed on the screen.

In Python, the "for loop" can be expressed differently to the one shown previously. Instead of having "for i in marks" where variable **i** in each loop is storing the **actual marks** from the array, we could have alternatively written "for i in range(len(marks)):". Here, variable **i**, in each loop, will store the **position number** 0,1,2 or 3 for the corresponding marks of 34,5,95, and 34. "len(marks)" gives us the number of elements (i.e., count) in the array "marks" which is count=4. Storing the position number instead of the actual value implies a change in the line "print(i)", as variable **i** is no longer storing the actual value of the array list. "print(i)" will change to "print(marks[i])"

Example 2 with a "while loop":

The same program was written this time with a "while loop":

```
marks=[34,5,95,34]
i=0
while i< len(marks):
    if marks[i]>90:
           print(marks[i])   # is executed only
if condition is met
    i=i+1 #is executed after if logic
```

Figure 4 while loop codes

The difference between a “while loop” and a “for loop” is that the “while loop” allows more flexibility to skip elements in your array according to your choice. For example, you can have conditions that will either skip by one element (i.e. i=i+1) or in other cases, by two elements (i.e. i=i+2). In a “for loop”, everything is restricted on one single line, e.g., “for i in range(len(marks)):”. With a for loop, you cannot change the sequence of execution.

5.5 Functions

Function is a concept in programming that allows you to reuse your codes at a different point in time in your program. Functions also allow you to structure your codes for a better visual representation.

For example, if you want to use different arrays to validate the different marks, you can use a function to structure your common codes and then reuse the same function each time you need to verify the highest mark with a different list.

```
def func_marks(marks): #grouping of codes
    for i in marks:
        if i>90:
            print(i)

marks=[34,5,95,34] # first array
func_marks(marks) #calling the function with
first list
marks=[60,87,98] # second array
func_marks(marks) # calling the same function
with a second list
```

Figure 5 function example

The above codes will print value 95 and 98 respectively on the user screen.

Function **func_marks** has been reused twice in the program. As you can see, the same code logic to check the marks, was not duplicated. To achieve this, two different arrays with two different sets of values were used as parameters or arguments to the function.

6 Twenty Questions:

Twenty questions are given in this section. For each question, the corresponding Python codes are written in a table. The expected result and a descriptive explanation are also given for each question.

The first fifteen questions consist of activities related to basic concepts of programming. The last five questions have more focused on developing your creative thinking and your self-learning skills.

Question 1: Loops only

Question 1 will show how a for loop can be used to repeat a sentence ten times.

Question 2-6: Loops and arrays

Question 2 consist of loop concept and conditional statement. Question 3 to 6 will read elements from an array sequentially and do some processing with each element read.

Question 7-8: Loops, arrays and if statements

Question 7 to 8 will read elements from an array but will perform a specific processing only if a condition is met.

Question 9-10: Ascending and Descending ordering

Question 9 to 10 will respectively show you how to order numbers in ascending form and descending form.

Question 11-13: Create sequence

Question 11 to 13 will show you how to create a sequence of numbers.

Question 14: Search a value

Question 14 will allow you to search a specific value in an array.

Question 15: Create a menu and its options

Question 15 will allow you to create a menu and navigate to its respective menu options.

Question 16: Modify a text file

Question 16 will show you an advanced concept in programming whereby you can read and modify a text file.

Question 17: Search a value in a text file

Question 17 will show you an advanced concept whereby you can learn how to search a specific value from a text file.

Question 18: Read, modify and write to a text file

Question 18 will show you how to update a file.

Question 19-20: Country-codes

Country-codes is a term used in this book to learn how to use functions, loops, and if-statements to plot dots on a screen to draw different objects. In this book, the map of Mauritius has been plotted in question 19 and the map of Rodrigues has been plotted in question 20. You can self-explore and make your own drawing.

Qu1. Create a program to display ten times, the sentence "I am working".

Table A Question 1

```
for i in range(0,10): # i starts with 0 and ends on 9
        print("I am working")
```

Expected Result	Explanation
The sentence "I am working" will be printed ten times on the screen	The variable i will change incrementally from value 0 to 9 from the first to the tenth loop.

Qu2. Create a program to increment a variable x from value 1 to 10. Your program should display the sentence "I am working" only when the variable value is 7.

Table B Question 2

```
for x in range(1,11): #i starts with 1 and ends on 10
    if x==7:
        print("I am working")
```

Expected Result	Explanation
"I am working" will be printed only one time when variable x is equal to 7	The variable x will incrementally change from value 1 to 10 and the condition will be met only when variable x has a value of 7.

Qu3. Create a program to count the number of items in the following list of numbers: 1,3,4,5,3, 4.

Table C Question 3

```
items=[1,3,4,5,3,4]
count=len(items)
print(count)
```

Expected Result	Explanation
6	The Python pre-defined function "len" will count the number of elements/values in the array "items."

Qu4. Create a program to display the values of the following list of numbers: 1,3,4,5,3, 4.

Table D Question 4

```
items=[1,3,4,5,3,4]
for i in items:
    print(i)
```

Expected Result	Explanation
1,3,4,5,3,4 will be printed on the screen (each on one single line)	Each element of the array "items" will be printed on the screen. These elements will be stored temporarily, one at a time, in the variable i on each executed loop.

Qu5. Create a program to calculate the sum of all values in the following list of numbers: 1,3,4,5,3, 4.

Table E Question 5

```
items_list=[1,3,4,5,3,4]
total=0
for i in items_list:
          total=total+i
print("The sum is ",total)
```

Expected Result	Explanation
The sum is 20	The Python program will loop through the 6 elements of the array "items_list" and perform a sum of each value retrieved. The sum will be added cumulatively in the variable "total". After completing the loop process, the program will print the final sum on the screen.

Qu6. Create a program to perform an average of all values in the following list of numbers: 1,3,4,5,3, 4.

Table F Question 6

```
items_list=[1,3,4,5,3,4]
total=0
for i in items_list:
  total=total+i
average=total/len(items_list)
print("The average is ",float(average))
```

Expected Result	Explanation
The average is 3.3333...	The Python program will loop through the 6 elements of the array "items_list" and perform a sum with each value retrieved. The sum will be added cumulatively in the variable "total". After completing the loop process, the program will perform an average calculation. The sum will be divided by the number of elements in the array "items_list". The Python pre-defined function "len" is used to get this count number. At the end of the program, the average value is printed. Float is a datatype that is used to work with decimal values.

Qu7. Create a program to search for the value "5" in the following list: 1,2,4,5,3, 4.

Table G Question 7

```
items_list=[1,3,4,5,3,4]
for i in items_list:
    if i==5:
        print("Value found=",i)
```

Expected Result	Explanation
Value found=5	The program will search for the value "5" from the "items_list" list.

Qu8. Create a program to count the number of occurrences of value "4" in the following list: 1,2,4,5,3, 4.

Table H Question 8

```
items_list=[1,3,4,5,3,4]
varc_occ=0
for i in items_list:
    if i==4:
        varc_occ=varc_occ+1

print("The number of occurrences for 4 is
",varc_occ)
```

Expected Result	Explanation
The number of occurrences for 4 is 2	varc_occ is a variable that will keep the count number when the value 4 is matched from the list.

Qu9. Create a program to sort, in ascending order, the following list of numbers: 1,3,4,5,3, 4.

Table I Question 9

```
items_list=[1,3,4,5,3,4]
varc_count = len(items_list)
  # Traverse through all array elements
for i in range(varc_count-1):
        for j in range(1, varc_count-i):
            if(items_list[j-1]> items_list[j]):
                var_temp = items_list[j-1]
```

```
                items_list[j-1] = items_list[j]
                items_list[j] = var_temp

for i in items_list:
        print(i)
```

Expected Result	Explanation
1,3,3,4,4,5 (each will be displayed on one single line)	The bubble sort algorithm was used. You can use any other algorithm that you prefer. To be able to sort values in an array, a temporary variable "var_temp" should be used to keep the previous value before new change in the current array position.

Qu10. Create a program to sort, in descending order, the following list of numbers: 1,3,4,5,3, 4.

Table J Question 10

```
items_list=[1,3,4,5,3,4]
varc_count = len(items_list)
  # Traverse through all array elements
for i in range(varc_count-1):
        for j in range(1, varc_count-i):
            if(items_list[j-1]< items_list[j]):
               var_temp = items_list[j-1]
               items_list[j-1] = items_list[j]
               items_list[j] = var_temp
for i in items_list:
        print(i)
```

Expected Result	Explanation
5,4,4,3,3,1 (each will be displayed on one single line)	The difference between the ascending and descending program lies in the greater (>) and less (<) sign notation.

Qu11. Create a program to complete the next two values in the following list: 1, 3, 5, ..., ...

Table K Question 11

```
x=1
var_list=""
for i in range(5):
    if i<4:
        var_list=var_list+str(x)+","
    else:
        var_list=var_list+str(x)
    x=x+2

print(var_list)
```

Expected Result	Explanation
1,3,5,7,9	The initial value of x is declared to be an integer number. To be able to concatenate the x integer value with a String, you will have to convert the value from integer into string value, with the Python pre-defined function str().

Qu12. Create a program to complete the next two values in the following list: 5, 10, 15, .., ..

Table L Question 12

```
x=5
var_list=""
for i in range(5):
    if i<4:
        var_list=var_list+str(x)+","
    else:
        var_list=var_list+str(x)
    x=x+5
print(var_list)
```

Expected Result	Explanation
5,10,15,20,25	Compared to the previous example, the variable x is initialized by integer 5. Inside the loop, it is being incremented by 5.

Qu13. Create a program to complete the next two values in the following list: 1000, 500, .., ..

Table M Question 13

```
x=1000
var_list=""
for i in range(4):
    if i<3:
        var_list=var_list+str(x)+","
    else:
        var_list=var_list+str(x)
    x=x/2
print(var_list)
```

Expected Result	Explanation
1000,500.0,250.0,125.0	The new value retrieved from the element will be divided by 2 in each loop. The new value will be added to a variable “var_list” and printed at the end of the program.

Qu14. Search for Rita and its position number from the given list: John, Rita, JIRA

Table N Question 14

```
items_list=["John","Rita","JIRA"]
var_count=0
for i in items_list:
    var_count=var_count+1
    if i=="Rita":
        print("Found item ",i, "at position
",var_count)
```

Expected Result	Explanation
Found item Rita at position 2	Display the matching value and its position in the given list.

Qu15. A program has the following menu:

1. Addition of two numbers
2. Multiplication of two numbers
3. Exit

a) Create a program to show the above menu:

```
print("1.Addition of two numbers")
print("2.Multiplication of two numbers")
print ("3.Exit")
```

Figure 6 self-taught on menu options

b) Create a program to request a user to perform an addition:

```
import sys
print("1.Addition of two numbers")
print("2.Multiplication of two numbers")
print ("3.Exit")
option=int(input("Your option:"))

if option==1:
    num1=int(input("Enter number 1:"))
    num2=int(input("Enter number 2:"))
    result=num1+num2
    print(result)
elif option==2:
    num1=int(input("Enter number 1:"))
    num2=int(input("Enter number 2:"))
    result=num1*num2
    print(result)
else:
    sys.exit(0)
```

Figure 7 self-taught on menu options implementation

c) Show how you can improve your current program with a loop functionality:

```
import sys
while (1):
    print("1.Addition of two numbers")
    print("2.Multiplication of two numbers")
    print ("3.Exit")
    option=int(input("Your option:"))
    if option==1:
        num1=int(input("Enter number 1:"))
        num2=int(input("Enter number 2:"))
        result=num1+num2
        print(result)
    elif option==2:
        num1=int(input("Enter number 1:"))
        num2=int(input("Enter number 2:"))
        result=num1*num2
        print(result)
    else:
        sys.exit(0)
```

Figure 8 self-taught loop improvement

d) Improve part (c) by using a function.

```
import sys
def func_main(num1,num2):
    print("1.Addition of two numbers")
    print("2.Multiplication of two numbers")
    print ("3.Exit")
    option=int(input("Your option:"))
    if option==1:
        result=num1+num2
        print(result)
    elif option==2:
        result=num1*num2
        print(result)
    else:
        sys.exit(0)
while (1):
   num1=int(input("Enter number 1:"))
   num2=int(input("Enter number 2:"))
   func_main(num1,num2)
```

Figure 9 self-taught on improving menu with functions

Qu16. Write a program to change the content of a file, **demo.txt**, with the keyword "change". Afterwards, read the content of the file (You need to create demo.txt file before executing).

```
f = open("demo.txt", "a")
f.write("change")
f.close()

#open and read the file after the appending:
f = open("demo.txt", "r")
print(f.read())
```

Figure 10 self-taught on advanced concepts on files

The following figure shows the content of a text file "demo1.txt" containing student information. The id of the student, the first name, the last name, and the English marks of each student are stored in this text file. Use the following figure to answer questions 17 and 18. You need to create the demo1.txt file with the following data before executing question 17 and 18:

```
demo1.txt - Notepad
File Edit Format View Help
studentid,FirstName,LastName,Marks
12,John,Rama,34
13,Rohit,Ram,45
14,Lina,Moree,56
```

Figure 11 content of demo1.txt text file

Qu17. Write a program to search for the student "John" in the text file demo1.txt. When the keyword is matched, the program should display on screen "Found John".

```
f = open("demo1.txt", "r")
keyword="John"
for x in f:
    if (x.find(keyword))>0:
        print("Found ",x)
```

Figure 12 self-taught on searching in a file

Qu18. Read all the marks from the text file "demo1.txt" and load them into an array. You are required to compute the average numbers of the values from the array. The final average value should be written in another text file "newfile.txt" (You need to create demo1.txt file before executing).

```
total=0
count=0
f = open("demo1.txt", "r")
for x in f:
    if  count>0:
        mark = x.split(",")
        total=total+(int(mark[3]))
        print("Found",mark[3])
    count=count+1
average=total/count
f = open("newfile.txt", "a")
f.write(str(average))
f.close()
```

Figure 13 self-taught on writing to a file

Result: 33.75 printed in "newfile.txt"

Qu19. Country-codes: Mauritius (self-taught)

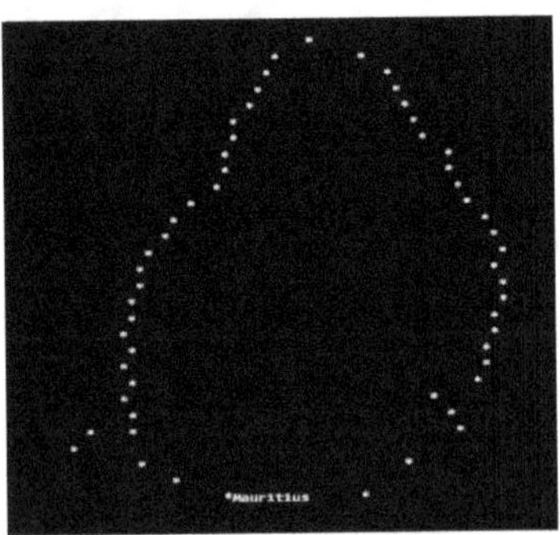

Figure 14 map of Mauritius at the end of the program

``
var_point="."
var_symbol="*"
def
draw(number1,number2,num
ber3,number4,val_word):
    val1=""
    val2=""
    val3=""
    val4=""
    for x in
range(number1):
        val1=val1+" "
    for x in
range(number2):
        val2=val2+" "
    for x in
range(number3):
        val3=val3+" "
    for x in
range(number4):
        val4=val4+" "
    val1=val1+var_symbol
    if number2>0:
 	
val2=val2+var_symbol
    if number3>0:
 	
val3=val3+var_symbol
    if number4>0:
 	
val4=val4+var_symbol
    if val_word!="":
 	
val1=val1+val_word
 	
    return
val1+val2+val3+val4
#same line
``
	``
	point1=[]
	point2=[]
	point3=[]
	point4=[]
	word=[]
	#define point
	point1.append(80)
	point2.append(0)
	point3.append(0)
	point4.append(0)
	word.append("")
	
	point1.append(76)
	point2.append(9)
	point3.append(0)
	point4.append(0)
	word.append("")
	
	point1.append(75)
	point2.append(13)
	point3.append(0)
	point4.append(0)
	word.append("")
	``

Figure 15 Mauritius (1)	**Figure 16 Mauritius (2)**

```
point1.append(74)
point2.append(15)
point3.append(0)
point4.append(0)
word.append("")

point1.append(73)
point2.append(17)
point3.append(0)
point4.append(0)
word.append("")
```

```
point1.append(70)
point2.append(25)
point3.append(0)
point4.append(0)
word.append("")

point1.append(70)
point2.append(25)
point3.append(0)
point4.append(0)
word.append("")
```

point1.append(71) point2.append(20) point3.append(0) point4.append(0) word.append("") point1.append(71) point2.append(21) point3.append(0) point4.append(0) word.append("")	point1.append(69) point2.append(27) point3.append(0) point4.append(0) word.append("") point1.append(66) point2.append(31) point3.append(0) point4.append(0) word.append("")
Figure 17 Mauritius (3)	**Figure 18 Mauritius (4)**

point1.append(64) point2.append(35) point3.append(0) point4.append(0) word.append("") point1.append(63) point2.append(37) point3.append(0) point4.append(0) word.append("") point1.append(61) point2.append(40) point3.append(0) point4.append(0) word.append("") point1.append(60) point2.append(40) point3.append(0) point4.append(0) word.append("")	point1.append(60) point2.append(41) point3.append(0) point4.append(0) word.append("") point1.append(59) point2.append(42) point3.append(0) point4.append(0) word.append("") point1.append(59) point2.append(41) point3.append(0) point4.append(0) word.append("") point1.append(58) point2.append(42) point3.append(0) point4.append(0) word.append("")
Figure 19 Mauritius (5)	**Figure 20 Mauritius (6)**

point1.append(59) point2.append(40) point3.append(0) point4.append(0) word.append("")	point4.append(0) word.append("") point1.append(54) point2.append(4)

<pre>point1.append(58)
point2.append(41)
point3.append(0)
point4.append(0)
word.append("")
 	
point1.append(59)
point2.append(39)
point3.append(0)
point4.append(0)
word.append("")
 	
point1.append(58)
point2.append(35)
point3.append(0)
point4.append(0)
word.append("")
point1.append(59)
point2.append(36)
point3.append(0)</pre>
	<pre>point3.append(37)
	point4.append(0)
	word.append("")
	
	point1.append(52)
	point2.append(0)
	point3.append(0)
	point4.append(0)
	word.append("")
	
	point1.append(60)
	point2.append(30)
	point3.append(0)
	point4.append(0)
	word.append("")
	
	point1.append(64)
	point2.append(0)
	point3.append(0)
	point4.append(0)
	word.append("")</pre>

Figure 21 Mauritius (7)	**Figure 22 Mauritius (8)**

```
point1.append(70)
point2.append(6)
point3.append(0)
point4.append(0)
word.append("Mauritius")

count=len(point1)
occ=0
for x in range(count):
    print(draw(point1[occ],
    point2[occ],point3[occ],
    point4[occ],word[occ])) #same line
    occ=occ+1
```

Figure 23 Mauritius (9) – last part

Qu20. Country-codes: Rodrigues (self-taught)

Figure 24 map of Rodrigues at the end of the program

var_point="."
var_symbol="*"
def draw(number1,number2,number3,number4,val_word):
    val1=""
    val2=""
    val3=""
    val4=""
    for x in range(number1):
        val1=val1+" "
    for x in range(number2):
        val2=val2+" "
    for x in range(number3):
        val3=val3+" "
    for x in range(number4):
        val4=val4+" "
 	
val1=val1+var_symbol
    if number2>0:
 	
val2=val2+var_symbol
    if number3>0:
 	
val3=val3+var_symbol
    if number4>0:
	point1=[]
	point2=[]
	point3=[]
	point4=[]
	word=[]
	#define point
	start=100
	point1.append(start)
	point2.append(10)
	point3.append(0)
	point4.append(0)
	word.append("")
	
	sub=10
	point1.append(start-sub)
	point2.append(30)
	point3.append(0)
	point4.append(0)
	word.append("")

val4=val4+var_symbol return val1+val2+val3+val4	
Figure 25 Rodrigues (1)	**Figure 26 Rodrigues (2)**

sub=20 point1.append(start-sub) point2.append(47) point3.append(0) point4.append(0) word.append("") sub=15 point1.append(start-sub) point2.append(47) point3.append(0) point4.append(0) word.append("") sub=27 point1.append(start-sub) point2.append(58) point3.append(0) point4.append(0) word.append("") sub=34 point1.append(start-sub) point2.append(64) point3.append(0) point4.append(0) word.append("")	sub=37 point1.append(start-sub) point2.append(66) point3.append(0) point4.append(0) word.append("") sub=46 point1.append(start-sub) point2.append(77) point3.append(0) point4.append(0) word.append("") sub=51 point1.append(start-sub) point2.append(82) point3.append(0) point4.append(0) word.append("") sub=57 point1.append(start-sub) point2.append(87) point3.append(0) point4.append(0) word.append("")
Figure 27 Rodrigues (3)	**Figure 28 Rodrigues (4)**

sub=58 point1.append(start-sub) point2.append(85) point3.append(0) point4.append(0) word.append("")	sub=57 point1.append(41) point2.append(8) point3.append(37) point4.append(10) word.append("") sub=57

``` sub=58 point1.append(start- sub) point2.append(80) point3.append(0) point4.append(0) word.append("") sub=57 point1.append(39) point2.append(2) point3.append(10) point4.append(0) word.append("") sub=57 point1.append(39) point2.append(8) point3.append(5) point4.append(58) word.append("") point1.append(48) point2.append(21) point3.append(8) point4.append(0) word.append("") ```	``` point1.append(51) point2.append(0) point3.append(0) point4.append(0) word.append("") point1.append(54) point2.append(5) point3.append(7) point4.append(3) word.append("") point1.append(57) point2.append(15) point3.append(0) point4.append(0) word.append("") point1.append(59) point2.append(0) point3.append(0) point4.append(0) word.append("") ```
Figure 29 Rodrigues (5)	**Figure 30 Rodrigues (6)**

```
count=len(point1)
occ=0
for x in range(count):
      print(draw(point1[occ],point2[occ],
      point3[occ],point4[occ]
      ,word[occ])) #same line from print (..
      occ=occ+1
```

Figure 31 Rodrigues (7) – last part